Custom
HARLEY
MOTORCYCLE
ART

Timothy S. Remus

© 2001 by Timothy S. Remus

All rights reserved. No part of this publication may be reproduced or utilized in any form or by any means, electronic or mechanical, including photocopying, recording, or by any information storage and retrieval system, without prior written permission from the author. All photos and artwork are the property of the author or as otherwise credited.

The information in this work is true and complete to the best of our knowledge. However, all information is presented without any guarantee on the part of the author or publisher, who also disclaim any liability incurred in connection with the use of the information.

The author and publisher recognize that some words, model names, and designations, for example, mentioned herein are the property of the trademark holder. We use them for identification purposes only. This is not an official publication of any of the firms mentioned.

Design by Rachelle

ISBN 1-884089-58-5

Printed in Hong Kong

CARTECH® Inc.,
39966 Grand Avenue
North Branch, MN 55056
651-277-1200 or 800-551-4754 • FAX: 651-277-1203
www.cartechbooks.com

OVERSEAS DISTRIBUTION BY:

Brooklands Books Ltd.
P.O. BOX 146, Cobham, Surrey, KT11 1LG, England
Telephone 01932 865051 • FAX 01932 868803
www.brooklands-books.com

Brooklands Books Ltd.
1/81 Darley Street, P.O. Box 199, Mona Vale, NSW 2103, Australia
Telephone 2 9997 8428 • FAX 2 9997 5799

From the Author

Motorcycles have fascinated me since I saw my first Dresser on the highway. In high school I lusted after the little Hondas. On Saturdays I rode my Schwinn to the Triumph dealership where gleaming Bonnevilles sat on the floor, so close and yet so far away.

I'm still fascinated with the bikes — with what makes them run — but also with the people who conceive the design, who build them, and who paint them in such outrageous colors.

Working with Jon Kosmoski on two paint books brought me into contact not only with Jon, but with a whole group of extremely talented artists. I became the lucky one who photographed each step in a complex layout. Some painters talk in terms of color theory while others simply work from experience and intuition.

Mallard Teal would describe color combinations that sounded garish, but worked extremely well when applied to steel and aluminum. Like most of these artists, Mallard could see these colors and the finished tank and fenders in his head.

I have to thank Jon and Mallard and all the rest for teaching me what I know about paint, and for helping me appreciate all the work that goes into a great paint job.

Introduction

Like everything else around us, the world of custom Harley-Davidsons is changing at a faster and faster pace. Not just evolving, but re-inventing itself every few years. What was hot only two or three years ago is old hat today.

The new custom bikes sport huge engines with well over 100 horsepower, 6-speed transmissions and endless billet hardware polished to an eye-piercing shine. Each year there are more wheel designs, fender shapes, and complete frames for the prospective builder to choose.

Among all these changes and revolution there is one part of the bike-building business that's changed, and improved, faster than any other. That one thing, that one part of the artistic puzzle, is paint.

Whether it's a deep cobalt blue candy paint job covered with multiple coats of clear, or a complex multi-level series of skulls all peering out from under another "layer," the paint on the current crop of customs is nothing short of amazing. With a waiting list of paying customers, artists like Nancy Brooks, Vince Goodeve, and Andy Anderson create paint work that is both flawless in application and extremely creative in design.

About the time you see one or two really, really nice paint jobs and begin to think, "this is about as good as it gets" along comes another artist with another concept so wild and free it simply stops you in your tracks. Whether it's the realism and complexity of a Chris Cruise mural or a set of tattooed flames from Lenni Schwartz, the designs are fresh and exciting.

To quote bike-builder Donnie Smith, "The paint makes the bike." Without the wild paint these bikes might remain awesome and fast. However, they wouldn't be the bikes they are: a unique mix of art and mechanics; that perfect synergy that comes from combining bright colors and unique designs with huge V-Twin engines and 10-inch rear tires.

There is no shortage of talent in the world of custom motorcycles. The current popularity of custom bikes creates an opportunity for a group of talented artists, both old and new, to design and apply images of stunning beauty. From traditional flames and eagles to modern 3-D spears and ellipses, the designs themselves, as well as the color and pinstriping, are the best in the world. This is not folk-art, this is fine art applied to machines.

This book, then, is a celebration of all that talent and all those individuals who've learned to use color and tape and airbrush to produce art unlike anything we've seen before.

The sophistication of the bikes on these pages is a product of builders and painters, many of whom have nothing more than a high school or tech school education. The strength of their designs comes from commitment, passion, and a certain innate ability to see what works and what doesn't.

Though the base paint was done in the Cycle Fab shop, using House of Kolor materials, the graphics are the work of Nancy Brooks.

Built by Michael Ethier, this Dresser uses top-shelf components from Arlen Ness and outstanding paint from Bob Morin and Sylvain Beliveau to stand apart from the crowd. Good painters can easily create an illusion that fools all but the best detective. Case in point: the "stainless trim" that surrounds the windshield, created with the airbrush of the talented Mr. Beliveau. Looking like a refugee from a paint-ball competition, the big Dresser uses white and purple as the main colors with splats and runs of yellow. Even the engine was powder painted in multiple colors. Like everything else the bags are dripping with yellow paint and mechanical detail. The small chrome strips are hand-fabricated and held in from the backside by small screws. Note the purple seat, chrome filler stripes between the bags and the fender, and the bag-mounted turn signals.

It's difficult to tell which is brighter, the polished 80-cubic-inch V-Twin with Arlen Ness billet air cleaner, or the intense scalloped paint on the tank. Spoked 16-inch wheels at either end and abundant chrome give this Softail the look of a classic two wheeler. Like speed lines on an art-deco poster from 1928, the scallops on these tail-dragger fenders give the bike a sense of motion even while at rest.

Not all Softails are big twins. This creation from Bob McKay was built by hand and uses a Sportster engine and transmission package.

A simple design that works: yellow paint and silver scallops. Scallops provide a sense of motion and also make the bike seem longer than it really is. Even the wheels get the yellow paint treatment. Note the way the oil tank has been modified to blend with the frame.

With the right paint and design, even a bike as big as David Silvia's Road Glide can look svelte and flowing. All it takes is a little lowering, a lot of purple House of Kolor paint applied by Perewitz & Keene, and graphics by Nancy Brooks.

Built by Dave Perewitz for friend Larry Schelzi, this screamin' yellow Softail uses Jesse James fenders and stretched tanks, all bolted to a special one-off Perewitz frame.

Stretched tanks and yellow paint are the work of the Cycle Fab crew. Air cleaner is a Perewitz special with graphics by Nancy Brooks.

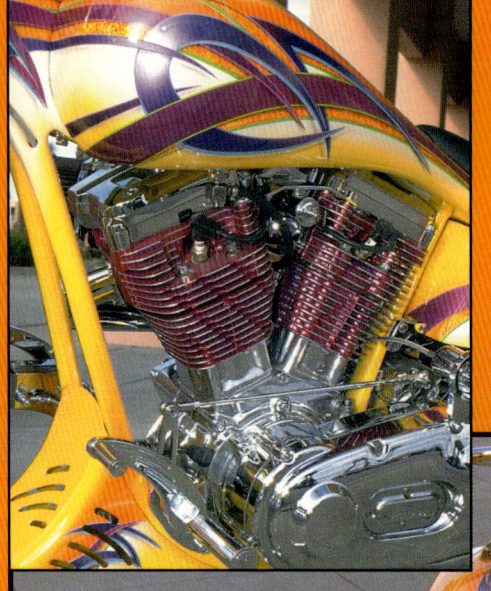

In building this Softail-style bike Andy Anderson set out to create "one piece" of two-wheeled mechanical art, rather than a tank and fenders bolted to a separate frame. With rough fabrication by Milwaukee Iron and help from his friend José, Andy designed and fit everything with such precision that all the parts blend together.

The rear fender isn't just a fender, but rather part of the rear body section, which in turn blends to become part of the gas tank. Once all the parts were fabricated and fit then the real work began.

The paint job was done on the assembled bike, rather than the pieces. First came the yellow basecoat then Andy's multi-step layout with fine-line tape. All graphic areas were sprayed first with a coat of silver basecoat, followed by multiple coats of Kandy colors from House of Kolor. Each spear and oval was created in multiple steps with slightly different colors that fade from one to another. Then came the shadows that lift the graphics up off the tank for a 3-D effect. All together, the paint job took over one month to complete.

Bob Belanger's BAGR is based on a 1995 Harley-Davidson Dresser. Body modifications are subtle and tasteful.

Note the small lip at the edge of the fairing, and the turn signals flush mounted below the chopped and smoked windshield. The modified fairing, stretched tank, and black paint are all the work of Cycle Fab.

Once the black paint was finished, the parts were all shipped to the shop of Nancy Brooks, who used templates and freehand airbrush work to create the colorful graphics. The last step in the painting process was the application of multiple clearcoats with sanding between each coat, designed to protect the graphics and create a perfectly smooth surface.

This Perewitz special uses a stretched Arlen Ness frame and 89-cubic-inch Evo engine. Don't look for speedometers, gas gauges, or air conditioning; Dave likes his bikes simple and clean.

Three-and-a-half-gallon fat bob tanks with long fabricated tails arch over the rocker boxes and reach back to meet the frame rails. One-off paint was mixed in the Cycle Fab shop with graphics by Roy Mason and Nancy Brooks.

Matt Hotch likes to use invisible fasteners to assemble his trademark bikes with that certain hot rod look. Most of the control and throttle cables have been made to disappear as well.

Part of the bike's aggressive look comes from the open belt, primary drive. The unusual abstract paint design is Matt's own, executed by Mike Shepherd.

The inspiration for Tank's Flight Deville came from a '39 Ford headlight and ring. With the light in hand a headlight nacelle was created. The wrap-around front fender, and fully enclosed rear body section were formed by hand from sheet steel. The gas tank is stretched to reach over the polished and painted 80-cubic-inch engine. Though it's difficult to tell, the bike started as a Harley-Davidson FXR. After finishing the bright pink paint, Tank created the cracked textured surface at the back of the fender. With stencil, airbrush, and green paint, he then painted a whole series of floating dinosaur eggs. Yes, the tail light is from a '59 Cadillac.

Not colors you see together everyday, Mallard Teal has a special knack for picking colors – and color combinations.

Harold Pontarelli used an aftermarket frame and 93-cubic-inch engine as the basis for this hand-built custom.

The paint job started with a basecoat of pearl white, followed by large panels of candy magenta. Then the scalloped areas were taped off and painted with a silver basecoat and various candy colors.

Here you can see the magenta "panel" and the smaller areas painted with candy blues over a silver base. Harold did all layout and painting, using materials from House of Kolor.

There are bright paint jobs, and then there are the paint jobs from Mallard Teal that make all the other bikes look like they're painted flat black. Paint materials are from PPG with pinstriping by Brian Truesdell.

A V-Twin engine is about all this Lil' John bike has in common with a seemingly similar model from Milwaukee. Instead of a stock frame, Lil' John used a fabricated chassis made from chrome-moly tubing – with an aluminum swingarm and integral brake caliper. Open primary and unique clutch are designed to be lighter and more compact than similar, stock components.

Steve Davis formed the gas tank and fenders by hand. While aluminum was used for the tank, steel is Steve's material of choice for motorcycle fenders. Dick Vale sprayed the very bright paint job using white as a dominant base with graphics in magenta, blue, orange, and gray.

An unusual Road King from Dave Perewitz, built for Kyle Petty and later auctioned off for charity. Note the bag tops designed to match the contour of the rear fender, the wrap-around front fender, and the small windshield.

The stretched gas tank is covered in magenta urethane from House of Kolor applied by the crew at Cycle Fab. Checkered flag graphics are the work of Keith Hanson.

With enormous talent and an unusual perspective, Cyril Huze creates theme bikes like this High Octane hot rod.

The engraving seen on the fork's lower legs and the caliper are what Cyril calls "tattoos."

The paint is a special one-off color that Cyril mixed up special using House of Kolor materials. Application is by Scott Sullivan. The High Octane logo and surrounding graphics are the work of Cyril and his wife, Brigitte LeJeloux.

Even the Arlen Ness headlight housing was painted purple with an engraved headlight ring and tattoo graphics.

A Road King with a difference: Paul Shadley painted much of what we commonly think of as chrome or polished parts, like the headlight nacelle and lower legs.

While the bike was apart, Paul had the neck raked an additional five degrees. Gas tank is stretched to meet the Danny Gray seat. Wild cherry paint is from House of Kolor, applied at the Shadley Brothers shop.

What really gives the bike its life is the bright colors splashed across the tank, bags, and fenders – all the work of Nancy Brooks.

Air cleaner shape is designed to mimic the shape of the extra long tank. All the body work, green paint, and even the graphics are done by the Tuff guy himself.

More work from Tank Tuff Cycles. The ape-hanger bars and fish-tail pipes give Gumby Glide a certain chopper-esque appeal. This one does without much chrome and polish. Even the rims are painted funky green.

The 89-cubic-inch engine is made up of aftermarket parts, including a set of Delkron cases, H-D cylinders and Edelbrock Heads. Paint color is kandy magenta from House of Kolor, applied at the Cycle Fab shop with graphics by Nancy Brooks.

Built by Dave Perewitz for Bobby Sullivan, this Roadster uses stretched tanks and Jesse James fenders, all carefully positioned on an aftermarket Softail frame.

Jeff Beebe built Home Wrecker in his spare time, thus the interesting name. The bike is designed to be a no-compromise hot rod with fat rear tire, left side brake, stretched frame, and 96-cubic-inch S&S engine.

Basic black covers all the sheet metal, including the extra long gas tank and the minimalist fenders. Both the black base paint and the extensive tattoos are the work of the Bootleg shop.

Webster defines a "Shovster" as: "A rare custom motorcycle combining a Sportster engine and transmission with Shovelhead cylinders and top end." This particular example of the rare breed is from the Shadley Brothers.

The unusual gas tank is from an early Sportster, decorated with some very high-performance graphics by Nancy Brooks.

far left
A Shovelhead cylinder and head, grafted to a Sportster bottom end, note the serial number, all set a-glow by the setting sun.

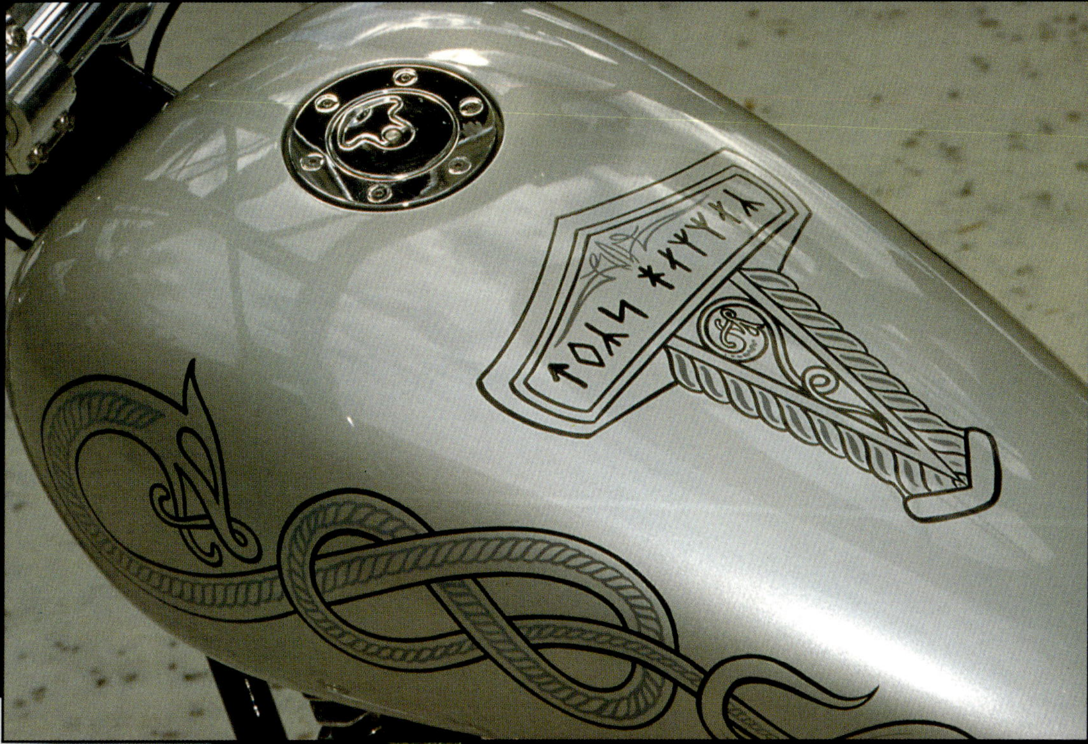

The silver paint is Frank's own, while the "graphics" are the work of Dennis Shephard – who reproduced Viking drawings that are over 1000 years old.

A true chopper from Frank Pedersen complete with "fifteen over" tube forks, hardtail frame, 230X15 rear tire on a 100 spoke rim assembly, and a tail light borrowed from a 1959 Caddy.

The extended tank, fabricated side covers, and Perewitz air cleaner all carry the unmistakable graphic designs of Nancy Brooks.

Joe Pro wanted an orange Road King, but not just any orange would do. The color seen here is tangelo from House of Kolor, sprayed by the Brothers Perewitz. While spraying they got a little carried away and painted things like the headlight nacelle and fork assembly, as well as the sheet metal.

One of the most interesting things about custom bikes is the sophistication of the designs. They aren't just sexy, most hang together as some of the best industrial art you're ever going to see – designed by a person without any degrees or letters after his or her name.

Busting out from inside the tank is this skull seen on one of the bikes from Bob McKay's Harley-Davidson.

Even the oil tank on the Bob McKay bike contains dead people trying to get out – created by the very talented Vince Goodeve.

Vince explains that all the work is done with airbrush at the McKay H-D facility where he works. "It's all basically free-flowing consciousness," explains Vince. "I just let things happen; nothing is a production deal."

A painter for 20 years, Vince has been working for Bob McKay for two years. Projects like this one take 60 to 90 hours for the airbrushing alone. Materials come from both PPG and House of Kolor.

Turbaned skulls, smiling skulls, unhappy skulls, skulls with an evil gleam in their eye, all from the very talented Scott Berosik.

The closer you get the more you see – the level of detail is truly astounding.

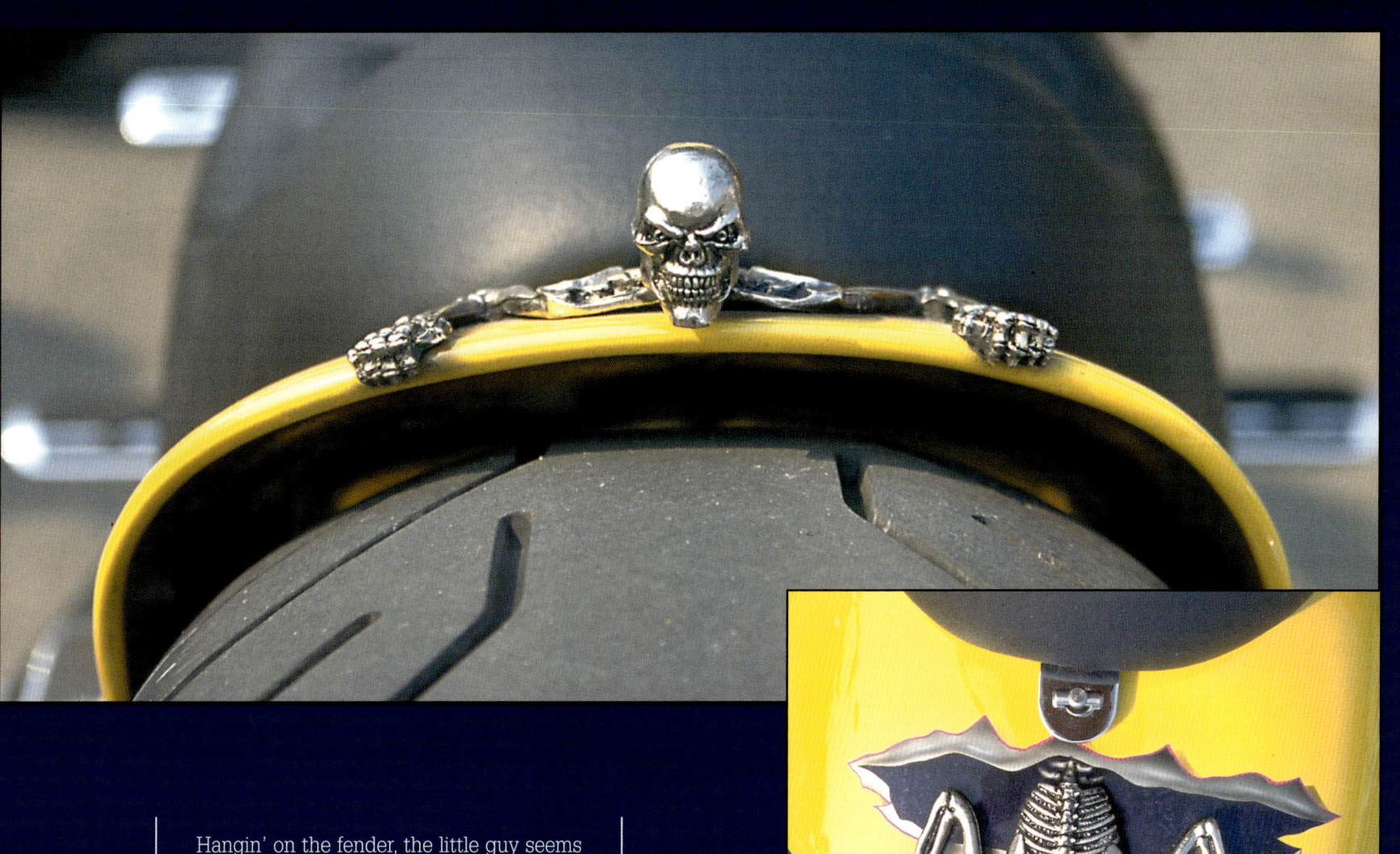

Hangin' on the fender, the little guy seems to have crawled right out to the metal itself.

Some people airbrush skulls and skeletons onto their bikes, and then some, like Bob McKay, opt for a skeleton in 3-D.

C. Romanstine

C. Romanstine

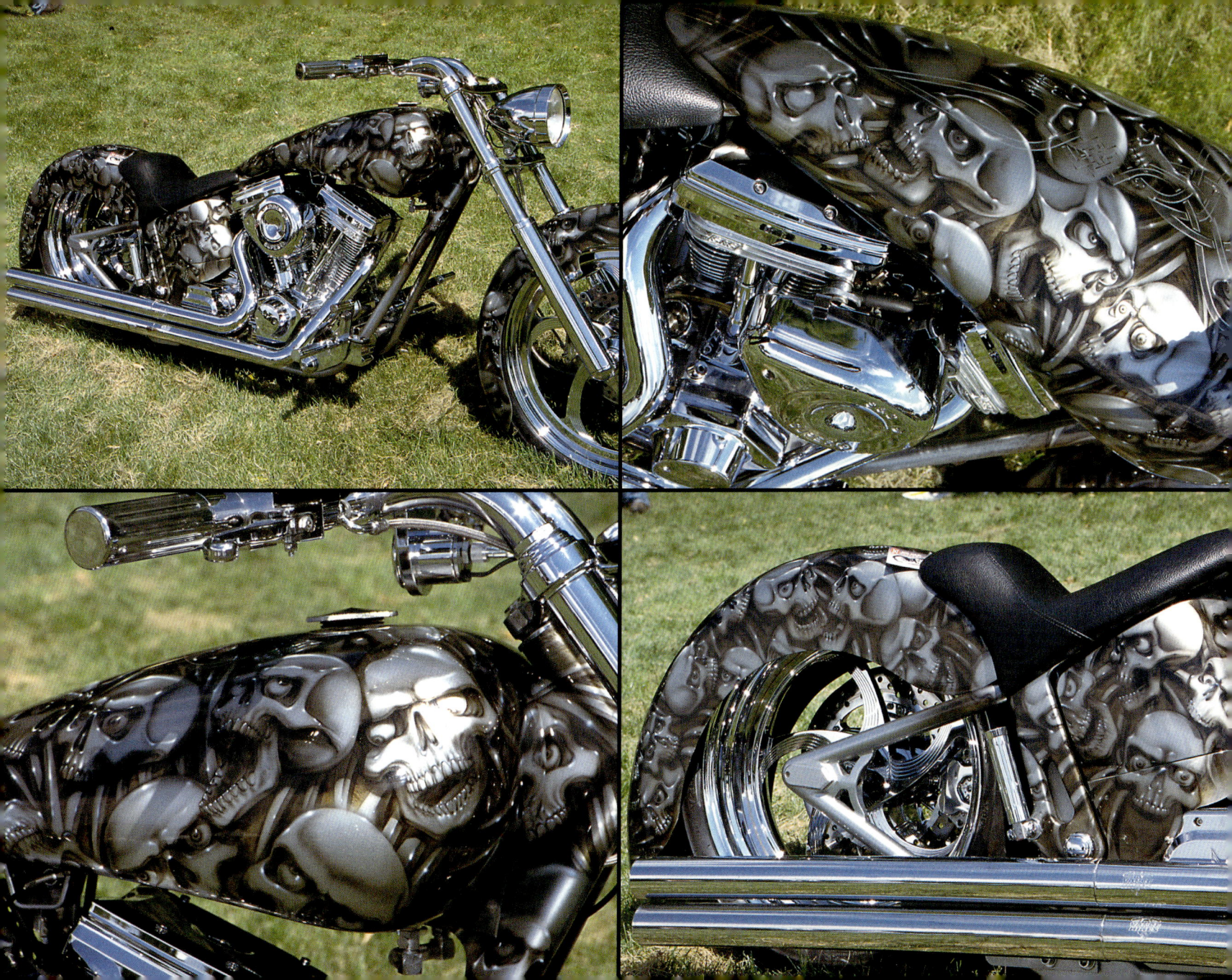

A unique mix of the two favorite graphic themes: skulls and flames.

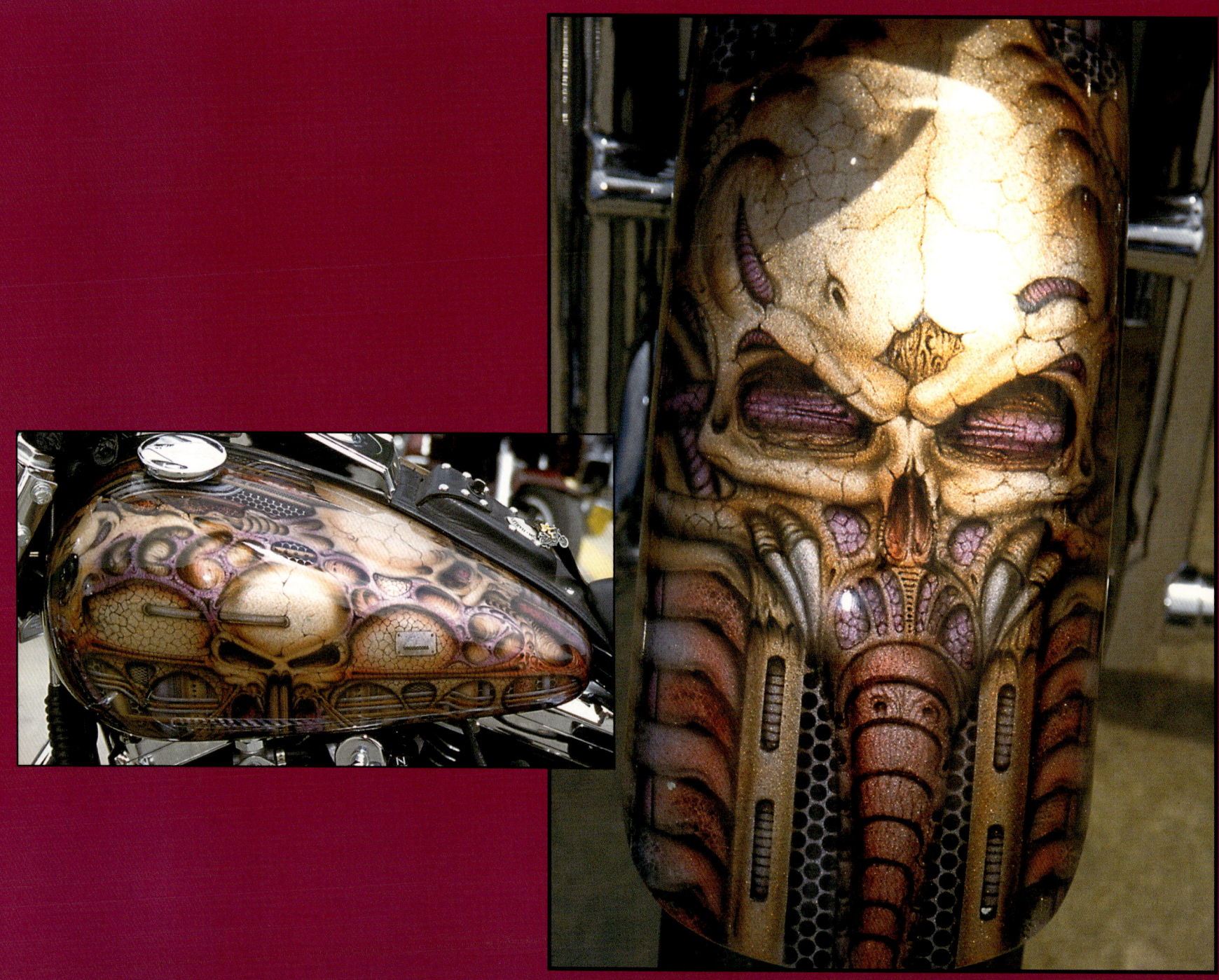

KEVIN SNELL

Perhaps this one is ridden by a biker/knight borrowing from both the seventeenth and the twenty-first century. Jousting on motorcycles anyone?

As interesting as the paint work are the designs, like this one that moves from skull to abstraction.

Sometimes what would seem at first to be too tacky or trite for words – tiger bikes and Elvis bikes and bikes covered with lizards – comes off as being quite amazing. The quality of the work and the way owners and artists add detail to integrate the paint into the overall machine transcends the standard categories. If art is anything that evokes emotion in the viewer then these machines are high art indeed.

Built by Dave Perewitz for Tommy D., this yellow Dyna uses an Arlen Ness frame and fully-detailed 96-inch S&S engine assembled by Jim Thompson. Stretched tank started out as a stock Dyna tank. Super bright yellow paint is from Cycle Fab, graphics and flying hamster by Nancy Brooks.

In building the black hardtail Bob McKay tried to combine the attitude and simplicity of the early choppers and hardtails with just a few modern conveniences like disc brakes and electric starting. The 3-1/4 gallon Sportster tank is emblazoned with a very energetic hog, the handiwork of Bevin Finlay.

The Sportster with the very nice image of eagles flying into a separate canyon is the work of Lynn Glaser.

The western theme saddle bag is the work of Chris Cruise…

…the same man responsible for the Cougar, Wolf, Grizzly portrait seen on the Tour Pak.

Like a small "project" that got out of hand, lizards and their bumpy skin embellish the entire motorcycle, even the air cleaner.

Leaping lizards, they're everywhere. And not just fabricated and stuck on top of the fender either (though that by itself would be enough work).

The lizards on K LARGO are made from the same metal that makes up the fenders and covers the tank.

The owner of this bike asked Chris to put on "all the species of Florida wildlife," including the manatee and otter.

Even the bobcat and the endangered Florida panther (not shown) are represented on the two-wheeled wildlife diorama.

Two-wheeled sculptures so visually arresting it wouldn't matter if they didn't run. The fact that they do run – and run hard – just provides another dimension to their appeal.

Old Shovelheads aren't obsolete yet, not as long as owners like Gilbert Quinn put designers like David Perewitz to work reinventing a classic Harley design. An appropriate design by Nancy Brooks: an American flag for an ex-police bike given a second life by the man who rode it new.

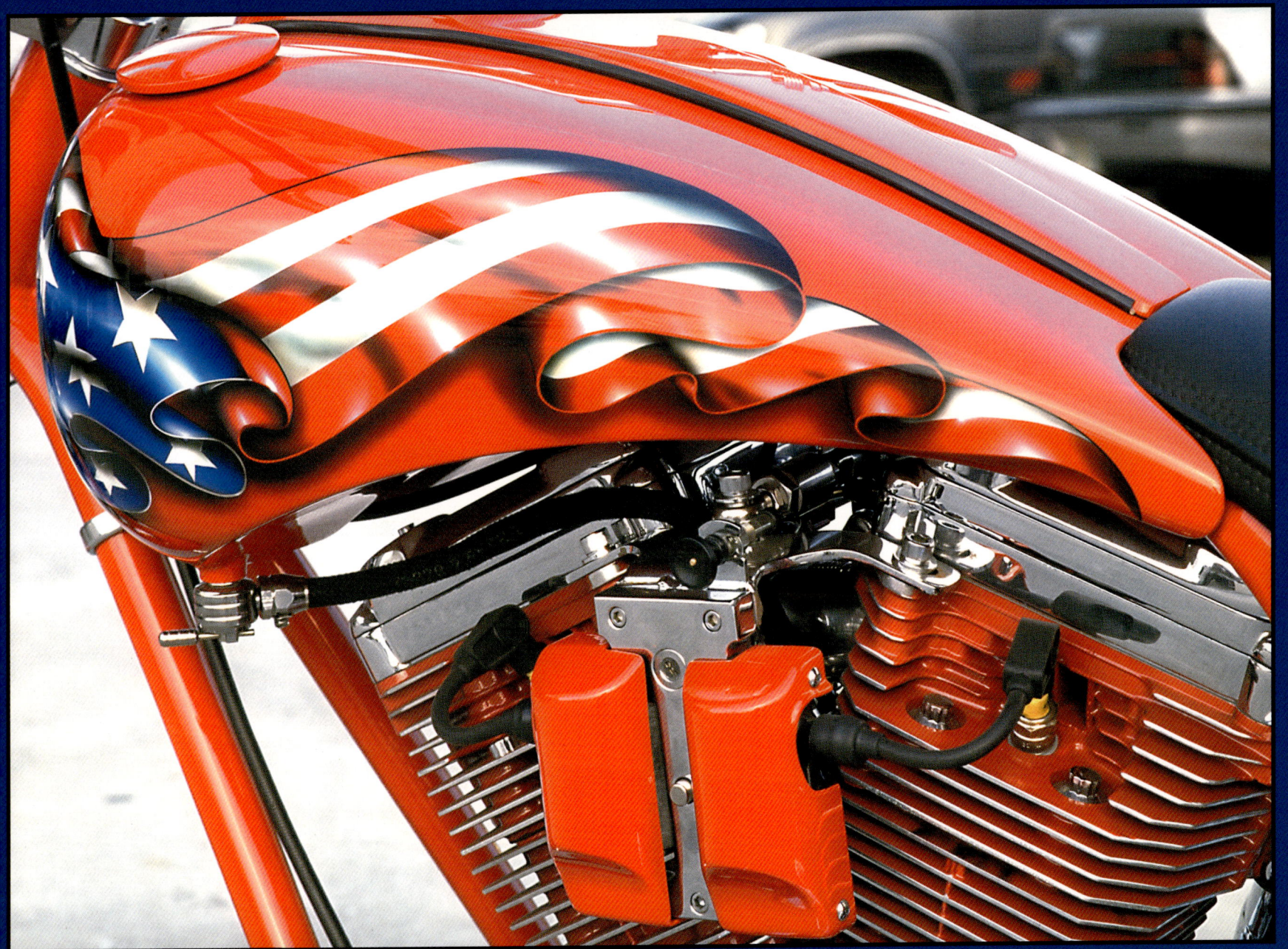
Nancy Brooks' flag is seen on an extra-long tank crafted by Cycle Fab for the Dave Perewitz FXR.

If building a custom bike is about having a bike that's your very own, then the bikes seen on these pages take that theme to a new level. Each one is a reflection of the owner's personality, ideas, and taste. A chance to say, "Look at me, this is who I am."

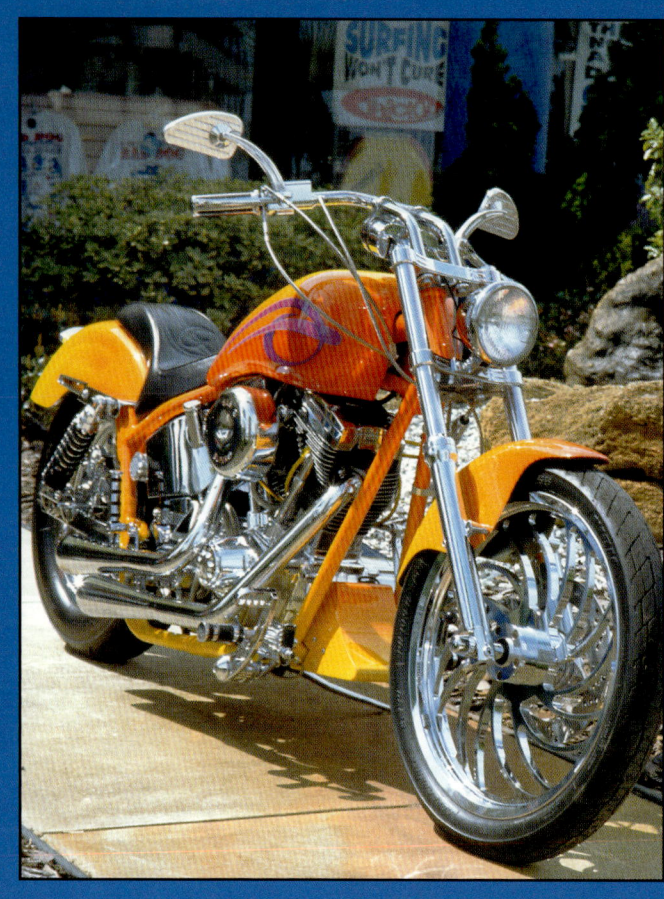

90

C. Romanstine

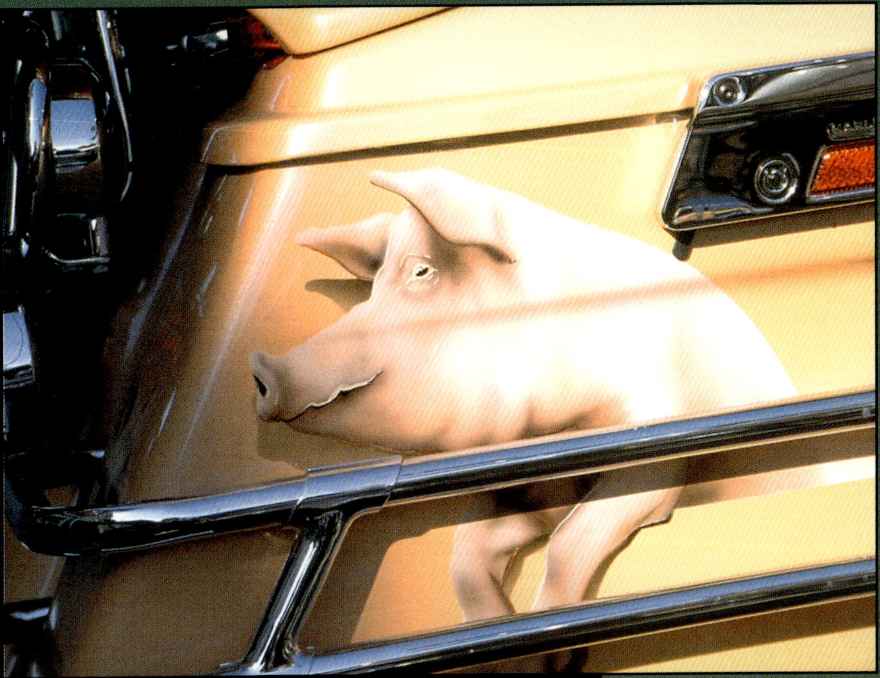

Anyone with enough money can go out and buy a new M-series BMW or million-dollar yacht. Yet only a few individuals can truly build a motorcycle of their very own, from parts crafted with old-world care, one at a time.

That's real gold on that Harley-Davidson engine, placed there at the request of builder Al Reichenbach. Gas tank was treated to the gold-leaf treatment while the engine cases were powder coated and then engraved.

Builder Terry McConnell calls this Dresser "A tasteful custom ... that won't look dated right away." The tail-dragger front fender nearly drags the ground while the gas tank stretches all the way back to meet the side covers. Bags with rounded tops help to give harmony to the design.

The paint job is as unusual as the bike itself. Sandstone and black, with a gray ellipse on both the tank and the bags. Even the lower legs and headlight nacelle are painted rather than plated.

Tank Ewsichek calls this a "stock Bagger with high heels and lipstick." Actually, his dressed out Dresser uses 17-inch wheels front and rear, along with lowering kits, to bring the big ride closer to the ground. Most interesting is Tank's split paint job and graphics package.

Not content to just paint the bike half red and half black, Tank taped off a line, then used a stencil and airbrush to create the Swiss-cheese effect where the two colors meet. The final touch is the seemingly random paint strokes.

Russ Tom at Downtown Harley-Davidson set out to build a very elegant Harley based on a Softail frame and wire wheels, with abundant chrome and polished aluminum.

With two-tone paint, Russ' machine takes on the look of a fine, old Packard or Buick Roadmaster. Damon's applied the burgundy over white pearl, with gold leaf used to good effect as a color break.

Tank art comes in all shapes and sizes. The art here is more of the metal-sculpture variety, as conceived by Bob Drone and executed by Steve Moal.

Instead of a painted tank, Bob asked Steve to make polished-aluminum covers for an existing tank. Seat pan is fabricated by hand. Note the abundant rivets used to lock in the heavy-metal theme.

Owned by Larry Page, this custom proves that sometimes less can be more. The pearl white paint job and white engine are offset by the mild graphics and the limited use of chrome and polish.

Custom bikes, at least the good ones, work on more than one level. At a distance the designs shout excitement. The color and chrome, the way the shapes blend from one to another, all serve to give enormous visual appeal. Examined up close, the shapes disappear. Viewers are left inspecting the incredible mechanical detail. The beauty of individual brackets milled from aluminum and held in place with chrome-plated, button-head Allen bolts.

Mike Marquart created this Un-Dresser to show just how clean and simple a big Harley can be. Flames are the work of Jon Kosmoski using House of Kolor Kameleon paint, which changes color under different lighting.

The Harley FXR line might seem passe, until you consider how right this FXR from Dave Perewitz looks. With 40 degrees of rake and the best flames this side of Hades, the bike exhibits a certain timeless appeal.

There are flames, and then there are FLAMES. These yellow on red licks with orange fades are some of the nicest flames ever laid down on a stretched gas tank.

Note the stretched tank and the way it meets the Danny Gray seat. Cylinders are painted red to match the bike and feature hexed and polished fins.

You don't need elaborate sheet metal or a million dollars' worth of chrome-plated parts to make a sexy motorcycle. Built by Kokesh MC outside Minneapolis, this little rigid includes only what you really need to go down the road with plenty of power and abundant visual appeal.

The super bright-red paint is kosmos red from House of Kolor, applied by painter Jerry Scherer. After the red was dry Jerry started the layout for the flames, painted with special one-off yellow paint mixed by Jon Kosmoski.

Built by Donnie Smith, this orange Softail uses a Daytec frame for the foundation and a S&S 113-cubic-inch engine for power. With engine assembly by Don Tima and sheet metal from Rob Roehl, this is one very fast, very sanitary motorcycle.

What most of us would call orange, is actually Tangelo from House of Kolor, applied by Brian Mahler. The modernist flames and pinstriping are the work of artist Lenni Schwartz.

An exception to the rule that FXRs make lousy choppers, Todd Markuson's green-flamed creation looks right at home with 21-inch front tire, ape-hanger bars, and sidemount license plate.

The tank is stock, except of course for the flush-mount cap and the great purple-on-green flames. The small aftermarket speedometer sits in a fabricated one-off stainless housing.

You might think that neon green would be bright enough for almost anyone, but Todd had to have more. Overlapping flames in two colors were laid out and sprayed by Lenni Schwartz.

By using a handmade swingarm with an Arlen Ness frame, Mark Shadley was able to run a 180 rear tire and locate the rear brake caliper on the left side.

Motive power comes from a Thompson-built 89-cubic-inch stroker. The base color is cobalt blue urethane from House of Kolor. Yellow and orange flame job is the work of Dave Perewitz.

Flames don't have to be red. Purples and blues work just fine on a black background with subtle pinstripe flames underneath. The clearcoats and polishing on a job like this means the paint job is complemented by the various reflections of clouds and sky.

Flames come in every size and color imaginable. These yellow fading to magenta are the work of Lenni Schwartz.

Built by Donnie Smith, this is one Sportster with the look and attitude of a big twin.

The ultimate in flames — flames in three dimensions.

In addition to the very complex paint job, each flame had to be cut from steel plate, then shaped, polished, and sent to the chrome plating shop.

The license plate says it all. Note the louvers with the tail and brake lights mounted underneath.

Rodney Roberts created the deep, rich rootbeer color by applying pearl red, then candy red over a black base with PPG materials. The orange and gold flames, and even the pinstriping, are Rodney's work as well.

In order to ensure his bike sat just right, Jerry Berryhill completely reshaped an aftermarket frame. Rather than raise the neck, Jerry stretched the top tube and kept the neck low, with a rake angle of 38 degrees. Chain drive is used between the 113-inch S&S engine and six-speed tranny, and also between the transmission and the 200-series rear tire.

―――――――――

Motorcycles, Harleys and V-twins in particular, carry with them a certain amount of built-in energy. They're sexy and exciting just sitting there. Radical paint and big-ass motors just add to the appeal.

―――――――――

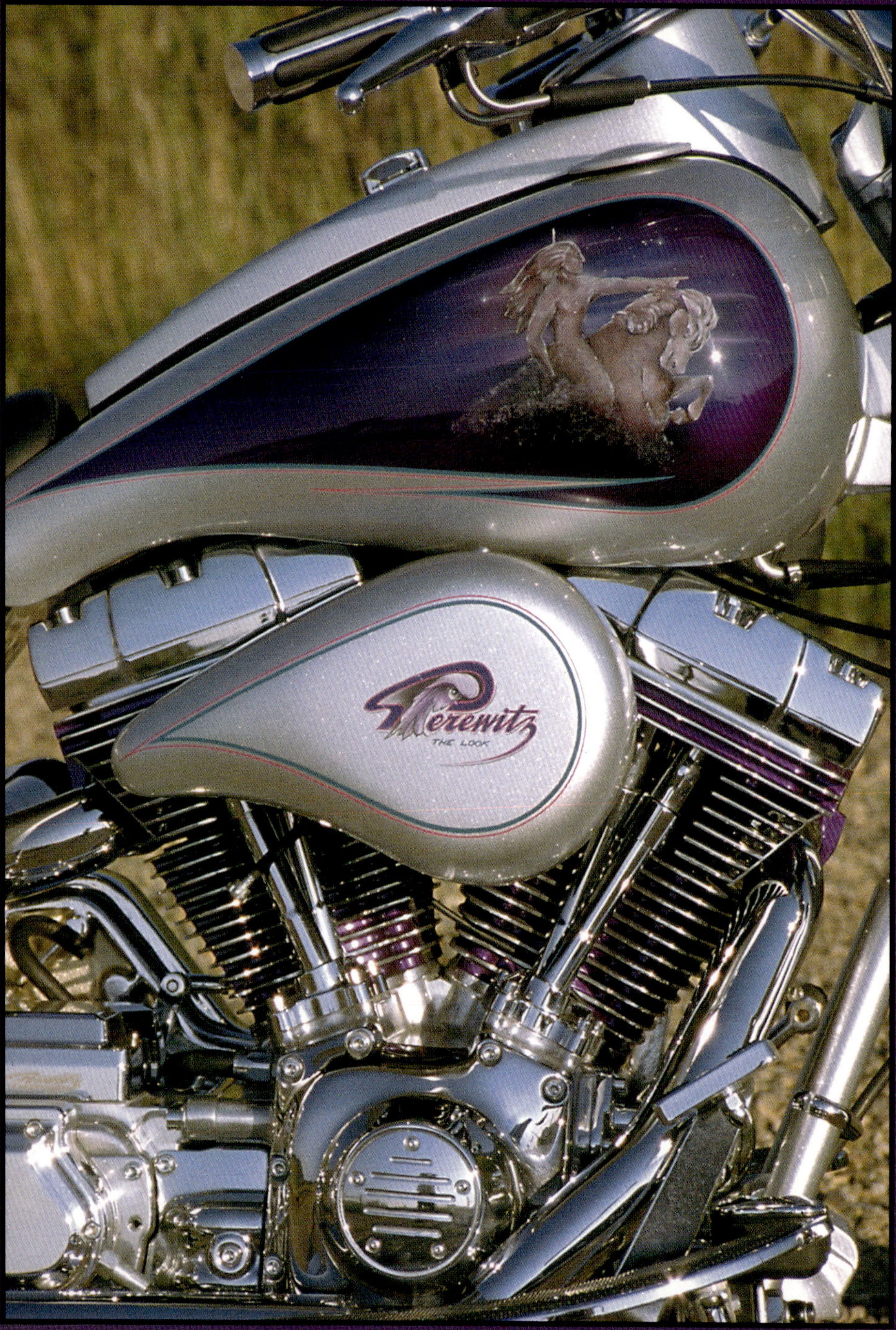
Perewitz
THE LOOK

"CRAZY HORSE"

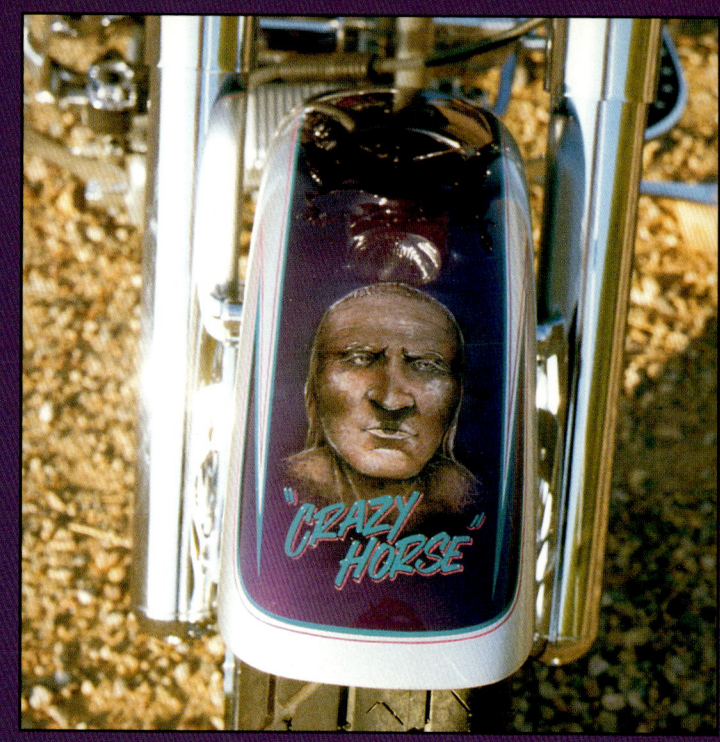

145

The paint work seen here and throughout the land of custom two wheelers is simply off the scale. Good enough to hang in a gallery, painted instead on a two-wheeled gallery for all to see.

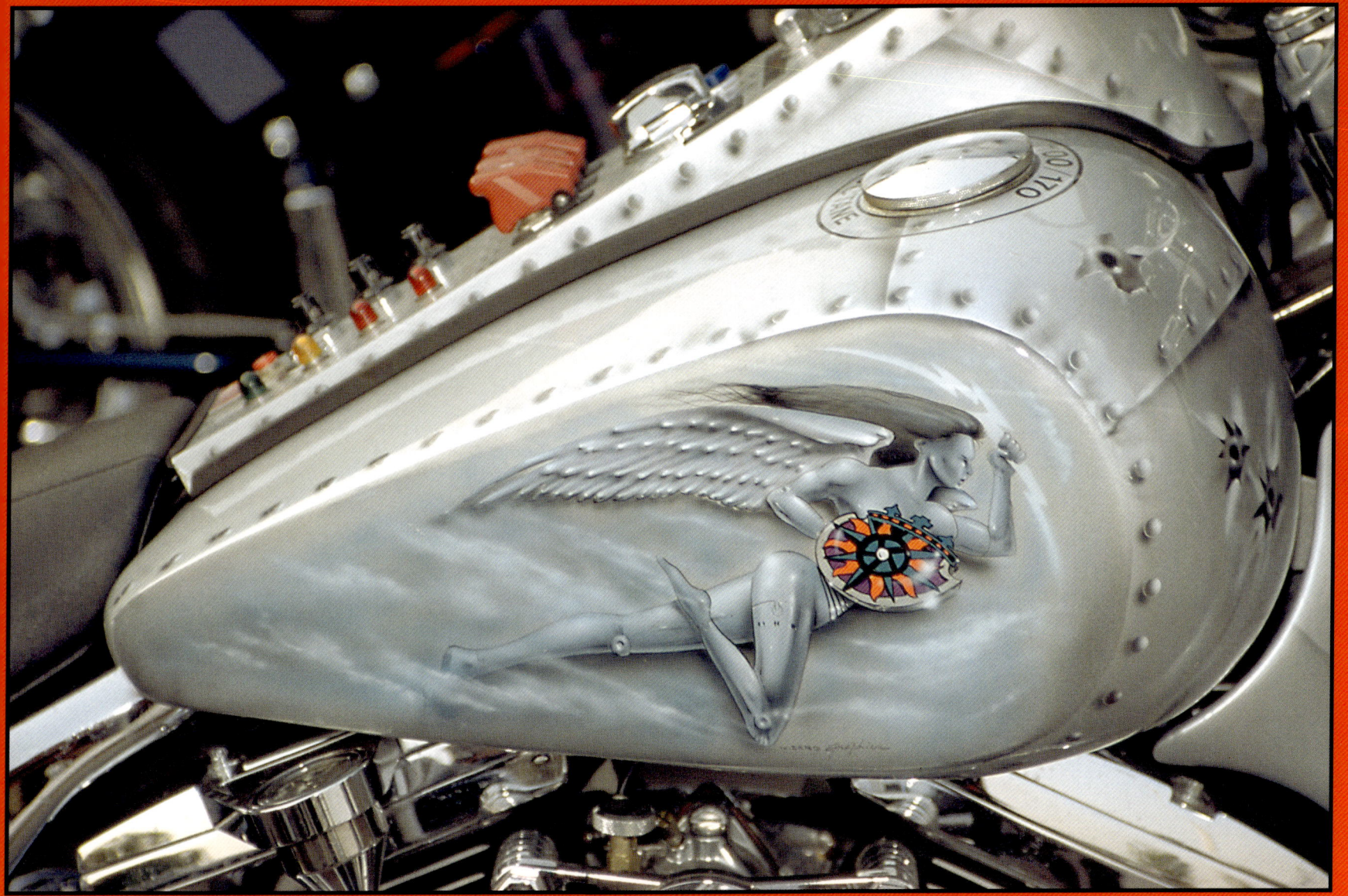

We are a society that accumulates possessions, most of which are designed by a team and assembled in a factory where hundreds roll off the assembly line every hour. We yearn for the honesty of hand-crafted machinery built to the highest standard possible. Custom motorcycles are all this and more.

Each Bomber Bike carries unique nose art on either side of the gas tank.

Another just-completed paint job, Miss Behavin' will have a lot of men lookin' for someone to misbehave with.

Like all the bikes in this series, the nose art on Problem Child is the flawless work of airbrush artist Dawne Holmes. Like all the others, this art is buried under a series of urethane clearcoats to protect the unique image.

Recently out of the paint booth, the name Lucky Strike brings to mind images of ex-GIs dressed in jeans and greasy T-shirts, with the requisite pack of Luckys (or Camels) wrapped in the left shirt sleeve. The aviation goggles are a nice touch!

The small Warbird fairing from Corbin lends itself to the WWII nose-art themes as seen here.

Another warbird from Corbin, complete with airbrushed panels, rivets, bullet holes, and a pin-up.

The base military gray paint is the work of Tom Rad. The paneled effect, complete with rivets, is the airbrush work of Lenni Schwartz.

Even the solid-disc, 16-inch wheels appear to be made up of panels and rivets.

Assembled from scratch, this very military V-Twin assembled by Kokesh MC seems to be part motorcycle and part aircraft.

The bike uses very little chrome. In fact, some of the chrome parts were stripped and then painted. Note the "bomber jacket" collar on the custom Mark Milbrant seat.

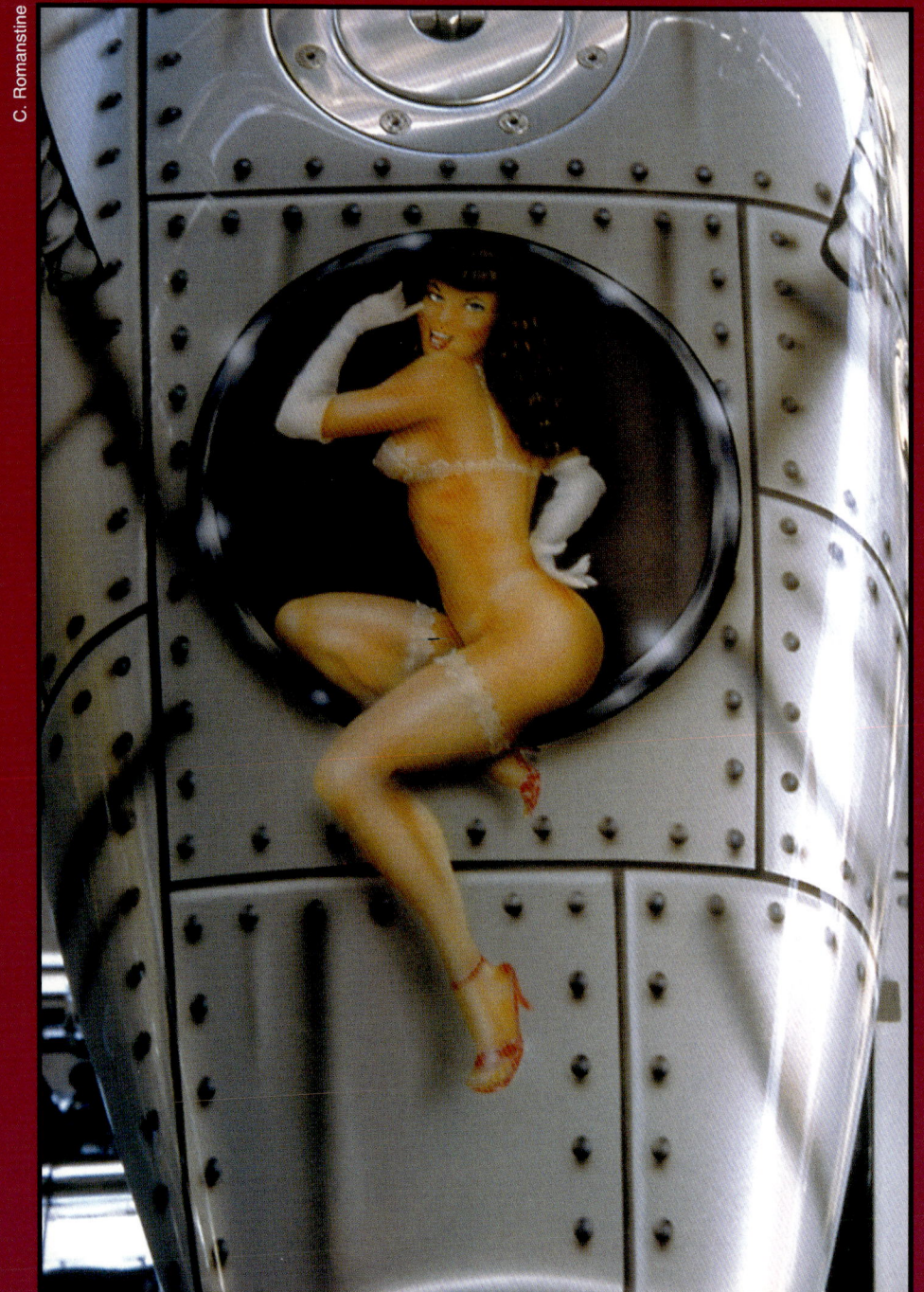